THE FUTURE OF CRYPTOCURRENCY? (2021 AND BEYOND)

THE OVERVIEW OF CURRENT AND FUTURE OF CRYPTOCURRENCY

MARK THOMAS

Copyright© 2021 Mark Thomas

All Right Reserved

THE FUTURE OF CRYPTOCURRENCY? (2021 AND BEYOND)

CHAPTER ONE

INTRODUCTION

WHAT IS THE FUTURE OF CRYPTOCURRENCY? (2021 AND BEYOND)

CHAPTER BY CHAPTER GUIDE

CHAPTER TWO

WHY IS BITCOIN'S PRICE DIVERSE THIS TIME?

CHAPTER THREE

WHAT ARE THE RISKS?

CHAPTER FOUR

5 CRUCIAL BITCOIN PREDICTIONS FOR 2021, FROM EXPERTS

1. **More Standard Acknowledgment**
2. **Rivalry From Big Tech**
3. **Rivalry From National Banks**
4. **Another Administrative Battleground**
5. **Proceeded With Unpredictability**

CHAPTER ONE

INTRODUCTION

Bitcoin is decentralized cash that utilizes distributed innovation, which empowers all capacities, for example, money issuance, exchange preparing, and confirmation to be completed aggregately by the network.6 While this decentralization renders Bitcoin freed from government control or impediment, the flipside is that there is no central situation to ensure that things run effectively or to back the assessment of a Bitcoin. Bitcoins are made carefully through a "mining" measure that requires incredible PCs to settle complex calculations and do the math. They are right now made at the pace of 25 Bitcoins at regular intervals and will be covered at 21 million, a level that is relied upon to be reached in 2140.7☐

These attributes make Bitcoin generally unique in relation to fiat cash, which is supported by the full confidence and credit of its administration. Fiat money issuance is an exceptionally concentrated action directed by a country's national bank. While the bank directs the measure of money given as per its financial approach targets, there is hypothetically no maximum cutoff to the measure of such cash issuance. Moreover, neighborhood cash stores are by and large safeguarded against bank disappointments by an administrative body. Bitcoin, on the other hand, has no such assistance frameworks. The estimation of a Bitcoin is completely reliant on the thing financial specialists are happy to pay for it at a point as expected. Too, if a Bitcoin trade creases up, customers with Bitcoin adjusts have no response to get them back.

What Is The Future Of Cryptocurrency? (2021 And Beyond)

What does digital currency's previous enlighten us concerning cryptographic money's future?

Chapter by chapter guide

- Why Is Bitcoin's Price Diverse This Time?

- What Are The Risks?

Contingent upon who you get some information about the eventual fate of cryptographic money, you'll find an alternate solution. A few investigators appear to be worried about the dangers that lie ahead, while others are sure that digital money has a steady job in our future.

Confident people may have a valid justification to keep up their uplifting viewpoint. Notwithstanding the COVID pandemic and the entirety of the financial turmoil we've encountered for the current year, Bitcoin's mid-November 2020 run has outperformed all assumptions, and the digital money is moving toward its untouched high. Since December of a year ago, Bitcoin has dramatically increased its worth, and some accept this is only the start of a long bullish run.

CHAPTER TWO

Why Is Bitcoin's Price Diverse This Time?

Various specialists accept that the current Bitcoin flood (November 2020) bears little likeness to its December 2017 notorious spike, when the cash broke every single past record.

The individuals who hurried into the unbelievable Bitcoin rally of the colder time of the year of 2017 were disillusioned when the money slammed not long after. In any case, many accept that the past flood was generally encouraged by singular speculators, as opposed to institutional help in the cash. Right when individuals got the cash for out, Bitcoin's cost dove.

Nowadays, Bitcoin is being advanced and upheld by institutional financial specialists. Large establishments like Fidelity Investments, JP Morgan, and PayPal are stepping into the crypto space. Loyalty has its own advanced resource division, JPM has delivered its interior computerized token and PayPal will permit clients to pay through their crypto wallets beginning one year from now. In addition, huge Wall Street multifaceted investments folks like Paul Tudor Jones have favored Bitcoin. Jones has even recommended that Bitcoin will be the anchor to hold us down against approaching cash depreciation, as the job of the highest quality level during the 1970s.

In addition to the fact that they are supporting it by allowing others to get it, they are getting it themselves. Huge firms like Square and Galaxy Digital Holdings are really accumulating a great many dollars worth of Bitcoin. This is conceivably uplifting news, as it implies that Bitcoin holders at this meeting may be less enticed to sell since institutional ventures are typically not purchased with the expectation of making a fast benefit.

Another great sign about this run is that couple of appear to be focusing on Bitcoin's noteworthy development. In 2017, Bitcoin's floods appeared to rule features and discussion, which made it so numerous who had never thought about crypto started to contribute, planning to get rich. The craze was unreasonable and brought about the cost falling significantly.

This time around, information on Bitcoin's convention has sunk out of the spotlight, and is just being talked about by those profoundly engaged with crypto and really have faith later on for blockchain innovation and its boundless selection. Possibly there's no craze this time since some are unfortunate that another fall is practically around the bend. Or then again, maybe, in light of the fact that this bull run might be the genuine article.

Despite the fact that many are continuing with an alert, there's a great deal of hopefulness encompassing the eventual fate of cryptographic money in the new year and past. That being stated, there are a few dangers to consider.

CHAPTER THREE

What Are The Risks?

One of the significant dangers of Bitcoin is that it remains unbelievably unpredictable. It can shoot up over a brief period and shoot down surprisingly fast days, or even hours. In addition, there are security dangers that can emerge like a 51% assault, where excavators pick up dominant part control and upset exchanges.

Nonetheless, the new convergence of institutional interest, just as organizations like PayPal making purchasing Bitcoin more available to individuals everywhere in the world, implies that cryptographic money is turning into a more certain apparatus in our monetary future.

CHAPTER FOUR

5 Crucial Bitcoin Predictions For 2021, From Experts

This year has been a wild ride for anybody to put resources into, or even view, the bitcoin market. The world's most significant virtual cash in December exchanged at more than $23,000.

At the point when the U.S. initially started wrestling with Covid-19 toward the beginning of March, Bitcoin was beneath $4,000. For proprietors or vendors, it's a gut-contorting wellspring of gains and misfortunes. For those (like me) uninvolved, it's an engaging business sector show, with hints of envy and dazedness.

Notwithstanding that enormous bitcoin value change — in a for the most part upward heading — 2020 was likewise a time of relative development for cash that, all things considered, has just been exchanging for 10 years. From my roost as editorial manager of FIN, a fintech pamphlet, here are what I see as the critical bitcoin patterns in 2021:

1. More Standard Acknowledgment

Bitcoin's utilization in regular day to day existence has consistently had a chicken-egg issue: Very hardly any utilization or acknowledge it in light of the fact that ... for a certain something, not many utilize or acknowledge it.

Be that as it may, 2020 saw a striking advancement in bitcoin variation. Noticeable fintech organizations, from Square's venture of $50 million in bitcoin to PayPal permitting its clients to purchase and sell bitcoin, gave it a blessing.

In 2021, we'll probably observe an expansion of this standard grasp. Search for in any event one significant U.S. or then again European bank to declare some sort of framework where they either empower bitcoin buys or consent to hold advanced resources for their customers.

2. Rivalry From Big Tech

Whatever bitcoin may or not have achieved in its time of presence, it has constrained a great deal of large, worldwide elements to consider offering global computerized cash.

Each organization associated with the installment space comprehends not just that there is a business opportunity for computerized installments actually available for anyone, however, that installments including distinctive money markets have the most potential. That is on the grounds that presently such exchanges can require days to determine, and regularly include weighty expenses.

Bitcoin has illustrated, assuming embryonically, that a worldwide advanced money can significantly smooth out that cycle. This year, both Facebook and Google — organizations with an enormous worldwide arrive at that bitcoin can just dream of — pushed ahead with large advanced money plans.

Tech contributions like Facebook's Diem aren't actually equivalent to bitcoin, however, on the off chance that they begin to get on in 2021, they may eat a little into bitcoin's development.

3. Rivalry From National Banks

This year, the Bank for International Settlements gave a report and review showing that 80% of the world's national banks are dealing with some type of advanced cash.

China has taken the computerized money experimentation a lot farther than some other country. As of late, in the eastern Chinese city Suzhou, only west of Shanghai, a lottery was held in which 100,000 inhabitants each got 200 renminbi (about $30) by means of a computerized wallet. They were urged to connect their computerized money to their financial balances, and in the event that they didn't go through their advanced money inside half a month, it vanished — both incredible methods to propel the investigation.

As China pushes toward a cross-country variation of the advanced yuan, it is probably going to undermine interest in bitcoin and other free digital currencies. One year from now may see comparable analyses in different nations.

4. Another Administrative Battleground

President-elect Joe Biden's organization will have higher needs in its initial 90 days than controlling cryptographic money, and obviously, Congress' state of mind and skill regarding the matter is difficult to peruse.

The characteristic supposition will be that a Democratic organization will manage more severely than a Republican organization, yet some have declared that Biden will be "useful for cryptographic money."

Perhaps, yet bitcoin fans will in general ignore issues like obscurity and its expected use for misrepresentation; for controllers, those are intense concerns.

Biden's group may all around concoct a more thorough and

objective method of directing cryptographic money, yet I would not wager on any preference toward bitcoin specifically.

5. Proceeded With Unpredictability

Since the estimation of bitcoin isn't straightforwardly attached to any undeniable true wonder, (for example, financial or money related approach), it can acknowledge or deteriorate in manners that are difficult to anticipate or even clarify.

As a venture, this makes it difficult to prescribe for anybody planning to maintain a strategic distance from large misfortunes. Some state bitcoin could reach as high as $50,000 one year from now, and in spite of the fact that that appears to be extraordinary, it isn't feasible if speculators move cash from different resources into bitcoin.

Obviously, it is similarly conceivable that the cost will head the other way in 2021. The one thing that appears to be sure is that the wild ride of 2020 will be rehashed — so lock in.

www.ingramcontent.com/pod-product-compliance
Lightning Source LLC
Chambersburg PA
CBHW070907220526
45466CB00005B/2164